HOW TO MASTER CHATBOTS IN 60-MINUTES

GET YOUR TIME FREEDOM BACK TO GROW YOUR BUSINESS, FAST.

BY TARNA SADLER

"Some made history, let's go make the future."

-tarna

If you're new to the internet game, you can follow Tarna's secret formula on setting up your first bot in less than 60 minutes.

If you've been online for a while, you can use the later chapters of her book to explode an already profitable campaign.

You'll read case studies in this book that show how real people just like you have moved through the bot world at incredible speed. In fact, you may become the next highlight story Tarna brags about!!

-sean malone

ATTENTION: A Special Note about how this book was created.

Dear Entrepreneurs & Business Owners,

Thank you for claiming your copy of "How to Master Your Chatbot in 60-minutes" and Get Your Time Freedom Back to Grow Your Business. Fast

This book will teach you critical chatbots skills, tools, techniques and more that every Entrepreneur & Business Owner needs to understand and apply.

This book was originally created as a live interview.

That's why it reads as a conversation rather than a traditional "book" that talks "at" you.

I wanted you to feel as though I am talking "with" you, much like a close friend or relative.

I felt that creating the material this way would make it easier for you to grasp the topics and put them to use quickly, rather than wading through hundreds of pages.

So, relax.

Grab a pen or pencil and some paper to take notes.

And get ready to take your chatbot knowledge to the next level so you can understand how to master your chatbot in 60-minutes and get your time freedom back, so YOU can focus on GROWING your business.

Let's get started with using chatbots to grow your business right now...

Until next time, my friends, stay legendary,

Tarna Sadler

Normal Never Fit Us

TABLE OF CONTENTS

Foreword

"She did whhhaaaaat???" I exclaimed.

"When did she have time to do that?" I asked.

Melissa turned to me and said, "She's a beast!"

We sat there in amazement thinking how does someone run a multiple 6-figure business, run a family, homeschool her son, write a book, and create one of the most complex corporate agreements we've ever had, and help restructure our multiple 7 figure software business in less than 3 days...

Seems impossible right?

Well, that's Tarna.

We met about 2 years ago.

Melissa and I had just eclipsed our first million online but we were also killing ourselves with the workload.

Enter Tarna.   She came to us through a mutual acquaintance.

And before we had the chance to chit-chat, she started asking questions about how we were operating the business.

What I thought to be a 20 minute introduction turned into a 4 hour 'wrench on our business' growth conversation...

And as I'm sure you'd agree, whenever a shooting star appears it's most important to hang on to it for as long as possible, right?

That's how we feel about Tarna.

She's been a game-changing life-saver for us.

And the craziest part?

All the value she's provided into our business has come as fast as a speeding bullet.

In working with Tarna over the past year and a half we've been completely blown away by her work ethic, abilities to teach, and strengths of creating very simple systems that even an 8 yr-old could master.

What I'm most excited about is that you have a copy of this book in your hands.

See, when we got started with our personal bot scripts, we didn't have a manual.

It was trial by fire - and we got fired... by Facebook.

10 times to be exact. Yep. Not cool.

Lucky for you, Tarna has masterfully laid out the steps to becoming an expert bot builder in an easy to follow step by step blueprint in *Bot Scripts.*

You can literally start from zero and by the end you will have your own top performing bot to accommodate your new idea, or any new (or old) business you have.

Tarna has dedicated years of time to become a master of her crafts and has developed a skillset which she's transferred into the words of this book that will help you succeed no matter where you're starting from. And you can do it all based on what you already know, even if you don't feel confident just yet.

If you're new to the internet game, you can follow Tarna's secret formula on setting up your first bot in less than 60 minutes.

If you've been online for a while, you can use the later chapters of her book to explode an already profitable campaign.

You'll read case studies in this book that show how real people just like you have moved through the bot world at incredible speed. In fact, you may become the next highlight story Tarna brags about!!

Bots are relatively new and there aren't too many expert bot teachers out there - and definitely nobody like Tarna.

With this book, you no longer have to give your first born to any copy writers, rather, you have access to proven and tested scripts that will help you change everything in your business.

The financial and technical barriers have been removed so you can focus on sharing your message with the world.

People often ask us, "What's the *slight edge* we can use to help us explode our internet business faster than anything else?" My answer is that it takes discipline, a lot of determination, a willingness to learn quickly, and the ability to follow the step by step scripting from this book.

My friend, you hold in your hand the secret to 10x your business. So, read, absorb, apply, and enjoy the ride!

-sean & monster

Sean & Melissa Malone
The Original Power Couple!
"Experience Everything Together"

Meet Tarna Sadler

Tarna Sadler is an expert in chatbots whose accomplishments include:

Education:

- Went from A Multi-Six Figure Corporate Executive for Real Estate Investors to Entrepreneur in 4 Months
- Spent 17-years Teaching & Coaching Professionals
- Led and Operated Teams of Hundreds and Managed Billions of Dollars in Real Estate Operations
- Self-Taught Affiliate and Digital Marketer

Work History:

- Rookie Entrepreneur who made $40,000 in 90-days using her chatbot with fewer than 1000 subscribers
- Coached more than 300 aspiring Entrepreneurs in her 1st 12 months of entrepreneurship
- Grossed More Than $500,000 in Affiliate Sales in 14 months
- Taught 400+ students how to master their chatbot, escape the 9 to 5 rat race and travel the world... all without being a tech-expert or having any past experience online

Awards, Titles, and Designations:

- 7-time Messenger Content Champion in a large underground Entrepreneur community
- 6-time Leadership Award Winner throughout the State of California
- UC Davis University Digital Video Excellence Award Winner
- National Award Winner for Philanthropic & Affordable Housing Contributions

Personal Info:

- Being home and a full-time mom is my dream come true Earned her first Vice President title by the age of 26
- Was the youngest Vice President in the country at a company of 5000
- Loves lending a help hand to those in need
- Once picked the wrong coach and almost had to go back to work
- Thought her email list was going to see her through and turn her audience into buyers ...and thought wrong
- Tossed in the towel on a successful career to have time freedom and travel the world with her family

Before You Begin . . .

Most of what you need is instruction and encouragement from someone who has "been there and done that!" with how to master your chatbot in 60-minutes you'll have the tools to get your time back and focus your efforts on growing your business! You can go live your life... and know, "The Bot is in The Office!"

And as you can see, Mastering Chatbots expert, Tarna Sadler, is uniquely qualified to help you understand everything you need to know about using chatbots to grow your business!

So, let me ask?

What is the best salesperson in the world? A chatbot that works 24/7, can handle every conversation at once, and does NOT demand a paycheck.

In our 60-minute Master Your Chatbot course we cover: chatbot set up, broadcasting, growth tools, Facebook ad comment responses, and several other tips and tricks.

Script examples and pre-written messages are there for your immediate use.

You can pick and choose which script fits your business best.

Or, if you are just ready to get back to your business, reach out. We may have a certified chatbot builder ready to support your business' set-up.

www.TheBotIsInTheOffice.com

Welcome!

Hi everyone. Welcome to The Beginner's Guide, where you'll learn how to master your chatbot in 60 minutes, get your time freedom back and get back to GROWING your business... fast.

My name is Dustin Johnson, and today I'm talking with chatbot expert Tarna Sadler on how every entrepreneur and business owner can get started on the right track with mastering chatbots and obtain the best results.

Welcome Tarna Sadler.

Tarna is a well-known expert on the subject of master chatbots and has graciously consented to this interview.

She will share with us the beginner's guide, so every entrepreneur and business owner can understand how to get started, discover how to master your chatbot in 60 minutes, and get your time freedom back to focus on GROWING your business.

Tarna, thank you for, again, joining us on this live interview.

Let's just jump right in.

My first set of questions is about your background and experience in the field of mastering chatbots so the entrepreneurs in our audience can understand who you are, where you're coming from, and how you can relate to where they are right now.

Then we'll jump into the beginner's steps to success every entrepreneur and business owner needs to understand about how to get going in the right direction. Now.

Chapter One: Tarna Sadler, Your #1 Mastering Chatbots Expert

With hundreds of hours of hands-on training I have learned how to not only implement an effective chatbot for my business, but also the businesses of several other digital marketers, business owners and entrepreneur colleagues.

I am a part of an underground entrepreneur community where we rely heavily on email but as soon as I employed my chatbot and figured it out, our entire business was 10x'ed.

In 2016, I set out on my journey to finally become the entrepreneur and start my own business. I wanted the freedom of "online businesses" but did not know how. By 2017 I was fully plugged in and committed to escaping Corporate America.

I partnered with a group of other like-minded entrepreneurs who had a system that was "plug in play".

However, that system relied a lot on just emails, which emails are great, and emails serve their purpose, but now with 1.3 billion people being in Facebook Messenger things have changed.

Our messenger apps are typically the notifications we receive on our phone (more often than our emails anymore, too). So, I understood that I needed to start not only learning but mastering the chatbot but figure out how I could monetize it too.

Within about 90 days of us really understanding the tools and the benefits in our chatbot, we were able to make $40,000 for our family and this was still within our first year of becoming entrepreneurs.

Now that I have mastered it and we have learned several techniques, we now see the benefit of what it could do for different business owners.

Mark and I, we come from different backgrounds and cover a wide demographic of working professionals and business owners. He was a teacher and football coach, I was a traveling corporate executive.

Now that we understand the tools and how we can use this service within our entrepreneurship, we want to go back and help other business owners employ their chatbot and, as we often say, "You bot is in the office."

Yes, we say that tongue-in-cheek because we know that no matter what time somebody hits our landing pages or our

Facebook pages that our chatbot is going to respond immediately.

I can't wait to tell you more about how and where you can employ your chatbot to not only grow your customer audience but turn that audience into a customer.

I spent 17 years in the workforce and always dreamed of being a business owner and preparing for this time of our lives. Trying my best to learn how to communicate and transfer knowledge to people in the easiest manner.

Becoming an entrepreneur, no, it was not an overnight success. I had to work at it then, I had to work to gain some version of success...and it is still something that I work at every day.

It is something that I learn and something that I grow with and just like chatbots, we (all) will grow as this continues to evolve and as more and more people move from just using email as a method of communication and into messenger chatbots as well.

Chapter Two: Your First Step to Mastering Chatbots

If you're an entrepreneur or a business owner who wants to

- ... turn your messaging conversations into buyers, or...
- ... take buyers from your website or from your email list into a messaging conversation, where you can drip out information,
- ... just simply automate your communication,
- ... if you find yourself stuck in your messages all day and want your freedom back,
- ... if you want to just get your audience to your live webinar,
- ... want to share your eBook,
- ... want to get them to your blog or from your blog,
- ... want to get them to your YouTube channel,
- ... if you are a digital marketer, an online entrepreneur,
- ... if you are a business owner with a traditional brick-and-mortar business,
- ... if you are a service provide,
- ... mastering a chatbot is worth your time and worth your energy.

If you're looking to succeed with mastering chatbots, this brand-new book reveals how every entrepreneur can discover how to master it in 60 minutes and how to get your time freedom back so... you can FOCUS on growing your business, not just running it.

So, what is a chatbot?

A chatbot simply allows you to communicate with your customers inside messaging apps.

Why should you care?

Messaging apps covers a huge market. Currently, there are more than 1.3 billion monthly active users. And, we know that personal email is not where we spend most of our time.

The Harvard Business Review says that while email open rates are at 20%, messaging gets 98% open rates.

If you think in terms of how big your audience is and if 98% of them were hearing your message, how many more people in your audience would you turn into buyers?

The best way for you to take this first step is to determine what messaging chatbot service provider you would want to first learn.

You will want to consult different training videos or even different how-to guides for setting up only the chatbot.

Then as you master the basics, it will be time to master the beautiful parts that allow you to really AUTOMATE while providing your customer what they want.

Chatbots are the perfect combo of AI hitting our hands for quick, efficient, and everyday use.

Keep in mind, there are several different chat service providers. (You can do a quick internet search to see what some of those top ones are.)

I personally use Many Chat a lot. That has been my favorite of the ones that I have tried. Some of the bots are a little more user friendly in my opinion or a little more intuitive than some of the others.

However, just like any system or service or software, there are certainly those tricks of the trade and those little nuances that are helpful to know.

Finding good how-to videos, plugging into a community, or finding cohesive how-to guide will help you master your chatbot quickly.

You will see how convenient the chatbots are and how important it is to use them to their fullest potential. (Check out my examples, scripts and statistics at the end of this book.)

After I spent hours and hours of trying to figure out the chatbot...

After I spent days sending out the wrong messages at the wrong times....

I rolled up the skills I gained from hours upon hours of scouring how-to videos... and made a simplified video series for my coaching students. In 60-minutes, their chatbot is set up, the welcome message is firing, their ad comments are being responded to and, their audience is subscribed to a 12-day sequence to gain trust, establish credibility and take them through our buying process.

How long does this step take?

This step can take several hours, or it can be done very quickly. It really is dependent on the approach that you take.

If you go and scout videos and piece stuff together like me, well... it took me several hours and a number of attempts to master not only the setup, but then to understand how to grow my chatbot subscribers, how to communicate with them and how to NOT piss them off.

Then I had to learn how to drip out content to them, automate the entire sales and webinar process.

This allowed me to quickly communicate with my audience how they wanted, when they wanted and, let them complete the process on their own terms (even if "I" was technically guiding it).

To avoid getting stuck, make a small investment into your education and into your learning to learn from a trusted chatbot user and get back to growing your business as quickly as you can.

Chapter Three: The Next Step to Mastering Chatbots Success

Next, it is important to understand some practical examples of how a good chatbot could be used.

Say you are a fitness coach and, on your website, you directed your audience to a PDF of a few of your favorite workouts... what if, when your audience requested the PDF you could deliver it via messenger.... which, then gives you the opportunity to drip out little workout videos of valuable content, teaching and providing value...

(and remember, you are communicating with them.... where they are! When I finally stopped and thought to myself... Tarna, how much time do you spend in your PERSONAL email? Not much!)

... all while you build their trust and show them you know what you are doing in your niche.

Perhaps you would send tips for healthy eating habits, meal examples, recipes, more workout routines or techniques – the options are endless and apply to every business that is coming into, or is currently, thriving in the online space.

When you have a 98% open rate in messenger you can provide A LOT of value.

Build trust with your audience.

Serve them.

Then, if there was a coaching program or a training course that you offer, as that person gains trust with you, they are more likely to want to learn and buy more from you.

Also, marketers or online marketers, digital marketers, online entrepreneurs or even bloggers for any niche can use this.

Basically, if you have a social media following, you should have a chatbot (in your office) ;)

Say you are a Keto expert who wanted to teach people how to eat healthier, how to optimize the ketones that help them lose weight and gain mental clarity.

You could drip messages out to teach them what you want them to understand... and the order in which you want them to understand it.

Also, this will allow them to gain trust with you and then, invite them to either a Facebook group or even back to your email list or a webinar that you may have to teach them more about other offers you have or, to teach them about your more in-depth training/coaching that you may offer.

If you have a product, say for example, you are a health company or an athletic company, you could segment out your audience and then, send them tips tailored just for them.

As you establish trust and rapport you can offer products based on how they interact with your chatbot.

Once you really master this, you can even set up actions, but we'll talk more about that later. (Cool tricks that allow you to have the chatbot carry on other sequences based on the 'actions' they take with your chatbot.)

If you are a service provider, say for example,

- …you have pest control service business
- …or you teach people how to run Facebook ads
- …or you have a pool service
- …or a dog training service
- …or an info product, the chatbot is a powerful way to create a conversational sequence to introduce them to not only your knowledge, but then, also how to take the appropriate steps to learn more about what you do and how your service can benefit them.

What's the best way for you to take this step and how do you do it?

The best way for you to take this step is to have a strategy.

Here are the FIVE STEPS I follow:

Number One: Don't just create the chatbot because other businesses have, or because other entrepreneurs have.

Think of the ways that your customers need your information and how they could benefit from getting it.

Then, design your chatbot in the conversation around those specific needs.

Number Two: Consider your customer and the journey you wish to take them on.

Think about where your chatbot could fit into their buying process or into their learning process.

Do you need a different texture to your chatbot at different parts of the buying stages?

Or do you need it to just be more conversational and informative?

Or do you need it to just close the deals you prepped them for?

It really just depends on the customer's journey that you plan to take them on and whether you are working with a low-ticket offer, a high-ticket offer, a low-ticket product or a high-ticket product, a service or info product.

Number Three: Test what works. Be like a chatbot and learn from how your customers use your chatbot.

You will learn quickly that your customers like to push the buttons on your chatbot.

They feel like they can quickly interact with your chatbot without it being a person, where they might feel a little bit awkward or a little less forthcoming with communicating right away or asking any questions.

Play with your chatbot and remember that your chatbot is like AI meeting you at your keyboard and one of the easiest ways for us to interact with it right now.

You should always aim to constantly refine and improve your chatbot experience for your customers.

Watch the statistics that come back on your chatbot, they're really simple.

You can quickly see how many opened the chatbot, how many clicked on what button and then, if there were any other actions that they took after that, you can see exactly what they did.

For example, you can test a conversation focused message against a more menu-driven (multiple choice) message.

If you were to say, "What is the reason you are looking to start a business online?" You are asking them to think, share and be vulnerable – right up front. Most people have a hard time with admitting a short-coming, flaw or area where they desire growth. Give your customer some time to get to know you first.

Start with, "I am really pumped you asked for more information about how I mastered chatbots. Would it be ok if I sent you the information you asked about?" Reply 'yes', and I will get it right over to you.

That approach is keeping them in the forward moving pace they are already at. Do not stop them dead in their tracks and ask them to spill the beans... (at first, anyway).

You can put cool buttons at the bottom of the message for your customer to interact with (include colorful emojis) and collect then be sure to go back and look at who pushed what buttons. (See a few examples of my buttons in the back of this book.)

Number Four: Perfect the chatbot's voice. Chatbots are meant to be conversational, but the voice and the tone still needs to fit with your overall voice of your brand.

Think about that in a manner of your voice and your tone, if you were hanging out with one of your buds, how would you converse with them, how would you tell them about your business?

That is how you should interact in messenger. Even though it is your business message and your sales message, you are communicating with them in a very intimate environment.

You should be communicating in more of a note conversation form, not like an email.

Your messages should be real small and something that someone can quickly read without even having to move their screen.

Number Five: Write great scripts, think about all of the possible questions a customer might have and how they might ask them. Then, create a variety of answers, interactions and content messages and see how they work with your customers. (Examples in back of this book)

Chapter Four: A Key Step Where You'll Discover How to Master Your Chatbot in 60-minutes And Get Your Time Freedom Back to Grow Your Business.

Now that you've plugged your chatbot into your Facebook page, you have it set up on your landing page and you've selected your chatbot service provider, now you can start to use the tools.

A few examples are:

WELCOME MESSAGE: A welcome message, is sent should someone hit the 'send message' button on your business page.

When that person responds to the welcome message, they are subscribed to your chatbot.

If they do not respond, they are not subscribed to your chatbot.

The originally sent message will still remain in your conversation list, but until they respond – they will not be subscribed to your chatbot.

To increase responses, ask a question that would generate a one or a two-word response.

If you ask them something more open-ended in your welcome message, out of my split test, I have found that people are less likely to interact with you.

(Which will decrease your conversion ratios of people hitting your chatbot and getting all the cool information you are going to share with them.)

BROADCASTS: What is a broadcast? A broadcast is a quick message that you can send to all of your subscribers, or certain subscribers. (See the back of the book for examples of broadcast messages.)

Here are a few of the issues to keep in mind:

"Hey, we are going live on our Facebook business page."

"We're live right now on our Facebook business page, come say hi."

A broadcast could tell somebody, "We are doing a webinar tonight. Wanna save your seat?"

A broadcast can direct them back to a new post/ad to get quick interaction to increase reach. (And, hack how little the business pages are shown to our audience.)

I have shared my eBooks.

I have shared videos, audios, favorite inspirational videos – in other words, you can get so creative.

There are several other growth tools you can also use at the beginning stages of setting up your bot.

Another one of my very favorites, I run a lot of Facebook paid advertising and, in my advertising, I will ask my audience to comment on the post to learn more.

When they comment, my chatbot immediately replies for me! (My bot is ALWAYS in the office)

When that reply goes back, I ask them a forward-thinking question that would require a one or two-word response.

Most times I ask them, "would be okay if I sent the additional information that you were looking for?"

When they reply, "Yes," they are subscribed to the chatbot.

I send them the additional information they requested, and then follow up with them with something of value in 3-5 days.

Often, I use a 3-part video series that provides value, answer questions and introduces them to the offer I am looking to share.

The options of what you can do with your chatbot here....
Well, they are endless.

Really, it just depends on what kind of business you have
and what you want to do with it.

Think through the follow up sequence in the same manner
you would physically follow up, share information or close
a deal casually and in person.

BONUS: I have found several different split tests, several
different conversation techniques and there will be several
of them at the end of this book, available for you to look at
as guides to implement with your business.

If you get stuck on the step up, search You Tube for a video
that describes the set up in the service provider you are
using.

Also, we offer not only a community for Q&A's, but
ongoing coaching and mentoring.

We also offer a certification program for those who want
to not only learn bots, but then also offer that as a service
to other business owners and entrepreneurs.

Now that so many entrepreneurs and business owners
have such a better deliverability and open rate, more and
more companies are needing this.

(But most business owners see the set up as complicated and overwhelming.)

Or, just flat out do not want to spend their time learning something that just needs set up.

So, wherever you are in this spectrum, I hope you know that they are options out there for you, and please do not be afraid of this tool!

Chapter Five: The Next Steps for Beginner Entrepreneurs

There are lots of other tools that you can implement with your chatbot to not only continue to interact with your customers on a more efficient manner, but then really deliver the message to them that they're asking for.

You can set up drip sequences like you would in an email sequence.

You can capture pixel data with your chatbot.

You can even set up landing pages in the chatbot, so you don't have to have your own website or buy a bunch of domains for different offers.

I have done a number of landing pages in my chatbot service provider, where I can have videos play right away and the setup takes second.

I can then have them come right back and communicate with me in messenger and let them get to know me... without PMing and DMing... my life away.

I can have them get tons of more information about my business and our entrepreneurship community quickly without ever leaving Facebook.

PRO TIP: You are not on the newsfeed... so you can say what you need to say... ;)

You can also set up custom URLs within the chatbot, you can then plug in that URL in different places to track different information, send them to different landing pages and communicate different sales messages, again right there in messenger (without worrying about FB's compliance issues).

Even though they hit the URL, the window just pops up from the bottom of their screen and they stay right there in messenger and get the rest of your sales message IMMEDIATELY.

Some folks just don't like being taken off of Facebook, they want to stay right there, where they feel like their information is more protected and safe.

Something more recent, is that you can even connect your email accounts and you can connect email opt-ins to make sure that you are capturing your traffic in a space that you own.

We own our email list, we do not own those subscribers.

As you really master your chatbot, just remember there are so many other things you can do.

Once they're set up, they are setup and running…. and all you have to do is go in and change the message as your business grows.

Chapter Six: The Perfect Mindset for Entrepreneurs

Do not give up.

Know that being a business owner or being an entrepreneur, there are times, where you just simply have to be the one to figure things out.

There are other times, where you just simply need to be the one that makes the decision to say, "This is not worth my time to figure out," and you figure out how to outsource that task, or delegate that to the right person on your team.

Chatbots, entrepreneurship, business ownership... it is always evolving, always growing. Be ok with the change and seek to be the one... who brings changes, not the one that resists it.

On another note, about mindset, chatbot mindset (I shall say) ;)

When you set up your chatbot, make sure that you are comfortable knowing that it's an automated message.

If you try to disguise that from your audience, they're going to know, but if you just own it, your audience is going to be more comfortable interacting with it.

For example, my first message to my chatbot subscribers tells them that this is an automated message, so that I can be out and enjoying my sweet family right now, and if they want... I can teach them how to do that same thing.

I coach, and I spend my days teaching aspiring entrepreneurs how to escape the nine-to-five rat race and how to build a business online.

Through that journey, I have not only split tested with my own chatbot, but I have also worked with a lot of different students to help them implement their chatbots, start broadcasting and driving traffic to a webinar, but also how to use growth tools in a very simple manner.

Just know that there are simple ways to take in this information and don't feel as though you need to be some tech expert to figure this out.

It is just starting slow, taking one bite of the pie at a time and implementing this stuff as you go along.

Remember, with your chatbot that you want to share content and value.

This isn't just a place for you to sell, sell, sell.

Your audience wants you to communicate with them in messenger just as somebody else would, just as one of their friends or their family members would.

Don't make them think too hard, don't make them do too much.

Just ask them simple things and share content that they'll see as valuable.

Then, after you figure this all out, you'll be able to build your rapport with your audience, be able to plan ahead and schedule, get back to automating your business, duplicating your efforts and get back to IPAs.

No, I'm not talking about the IPA beers that some folks drink, I'm talking about INCOME PRODUCING ACTIVITIES.

Chapter Seven: Critical Advice When Getting Started with Mastering Chatbots

Starting a chatbot and building a subscriber list may sound daunting.

There may even be parts of this, where you're feeling, "I'm very overwhelmed," or you might even be feeling as, "Okay, I haven't learned a ton and I need to know more."

Whatever phase you're at, please know that you are awesome, and this growth will be fun. In no time you can be where you want to be.

You are so capable of getting this situated and figured out.

If you just start off with implementing and attaching the chatbot to your page and start getting subscribers, then you can learn how to communicate with them.

This is no different than if you were communicating with them in an email list or an email follow-up series. (Just a lot shorter, and way more conversational.)

Don't give up on yourself and know that it does just take the time to put the pieces into place.

Then, over time, you will be able to develop out your sequences and more.

You'll be able to attach actions and tags and really automate yourself and get out and...

- ... start living life
- ... growing your business
- ... and staying in those income producing activities because
- ...again, remember, "The Bot is in the Office". (And you don't have to be.)

Chapter Eight: Resources No Entrepreneur Should Be Without

There are a lot of confusing and dry videos out there that are difficult to execute from.

Just be aware of that when you start looking at the information.

At least, that is how it was for me when I started my "campaign" to figure out my chatbot and save our entrepreneurship.

You'll want to listen to the videos or watch it a few times and seek the concept they're trying to share with you.

Build on all the little techniques and basic set-up steps first.

That is what saved our butts.

We got in and "learned" the platform, then we "learned" the tools within the platform. It took us a lot of time to master all of the aspects.

And now that we have, I want to help other avoid the time it took for us.

Whether it is for a real estate entrepreneur, digital marketer entrepreneur, a fitness coach, or somebody who is looking to sell a training course online, we want to get you our scripts.

www.TheBotIsInTheOffice.com

Chapter Nine: Mastering Chatbots Time Wasters

You can get lost trying to figure out how and where to start. Then hit a pitfall when trying to figure out what to say.

It's best to just start out with a roadmap and know that it is okay to not know what you're doing when you first start out.

If you follow a good roadmap and build out good conversations, you'll be off and running with your chatbot in no time.

You'll be pleasantly surprised how much your audience will like interacting with your chatbot.

Oh, and, when you're sitting around, closing deals, working on finances, growing your business or out with a customer and you see somebody interacting with your chatbot...

You'll be sure to smile and know that you are NOT paying a person to respond to random messages.

You will be helping your customer immediately... while they are still in a "curious" or "ready to buy" mindset.

Oh, and you do not have your phone, or your laptop stuck in your hand, responding to messages ... either.

Where do I see some of us wasting a lot of time? **I see some of us wasting a lot of time by <u>not</u> implementing the use of a chatbot.**

Chapter Ten: The Top Mastering Chatbots Challenges Beginner Entrepreneur Face

Learning where to start I think is the hardest thing for entrepreneurs and business owners right now.

So, most times, they just don't start. They simply do not have the time to learn.

Another challenge I have seen with my 400 plus students is that they forget that they shouldn't be selling in every message and they forget to share content and value with their subscribers.

This is a very important concept.

If you want to get people to trust you in a world of big shiny things…you MUST provide value…and a lot of it.

Don't be afraid to over-deliver on value.

It will ALWAYS come back in a bigger way.

This is a very simple but often missed step in the relationship building process with your customer.

Try and give away for free, what others charge for.

Another thing is overusing it. That's another challenge I have seen with some of my students. You don't want to send more than one or two messages a week.

You do not want to bother your subscribers, they don't want to hear from you every day.

They are looking for value from people without even knowing it.

So, you want to make sure that you lead with carrot, carrot, carrot before you ask for anything.

Shoot to provide at least five to seven pieces of value before you ever were to ask for them to do something for you in return.

This will help prepare your customer to look forward to your messages.

Don't get caught up being the used-car salesman, who is constantly talking about the next best deal.

Also, remember that you can really create a two-way conversation.

You don't want your audience to always think you're just talking at them and just telling them what they should and shouldn't do.

Try to encourage some conversation and try to put some fun buttons on there, so that they're just likely to interact with it.

PRO TIP: Use emojis on your chatbot messages and on your chatbot buttons.

By the way, did you know, 5 billion emojis fly around messenger ... a day. That is insanity.

That means often, folks are using more than one emoji a day because there's only 1.3 billion active messenger users per month.

Don't be afraid to use a little bit of color, but don't overdo it either.

Consider your audience and think about how they communicate.

If you have a more mature audience, you might want to use fewer emojis. If you have a younger, racier audience, you might want to use more.

Chapter Eleven: Hidden Mastering Chatbots Opportunities

There are so many different ways you can use your chatbot. Don't mind me while I nerd out a little.

- Do you have a webinar that you invite your audience to? You can send out a webinar invite.
- You can also send out a calendar reminder for them to be reminder of your webinar.
- I love doing that!
- If your business provides a service or if you have customers that would turn in service tickets or a service request, you can set up your chatbot to take in the service request and notify an admin.
- You can direct them to a google form and collect survey type information.
- Provide video series.
- Direct them to your YouTube channel, your YouTube lives.
- Direct them to frequently asked questions.
- Use a landing page that is built by your chatbot... they even slide up from the bottom of their screen and play videos immediately.

I cannot wait to hear how you utilize the tools that are now available to us to enhance our customer reach.

How can we continue to reach our customer base without competing with bigger marketing budgets?

Messenger isn't going anywhere, and its users continue to climb every day. This is a tool that businesses WILL benefit from.

So, what can we do together to make sure... no one is late to the party?

Chapter Twelve: A Mastering Chatbots Case Study

About nine months into our entrepreneurship journey, we used an affiliate marketing program that sent out our emails.

On this journey, I made a mistake that many young entrepreneurs make...I had chosen the wrong coach. I had chosen somebody, who was not aligned with my morals or with my values.

We did not know it at the time. We sold our home, the frig, the washer and dryer and the big 3D TV. We went all in.

At first, things were okay, but after a back-end shift... things were not okay. That coach, well, they I guess, thought it was best to withhold the issue, instead of letting us figure out how to fix is.

As we were coming to the last few months of savings... I knew I had to figure something out... even if we were paying for a system "to do it for us".

That is when I learned how to master the chatbot and within 90 days our first broadcast, our family had recovered the business and made $40,000 by mastering our chatbot.

A few months into that is when I started coaching our digital community of entrepreneurs and teaching them how to master their chatbots…. The positive results grew and grew!

Alex, one of my students, had four high ticket buyers within 30 days of implementing these techniques.

Our high-ticket offer is $10,000. What could you do with four high ticket $10,000 sells in 30 days of implementing this information?

Within 21 days of us releasing that 4-part series, we had 32 students make high-ticket sales, and that number has not stopped climbing.

Mastering this tool didn't just save our business, it has helped build so many others' businesses.

Yes, we need emails. They still have their place. But, now that we have another tool… it is important to stay with the times and use all of the strategies we can.

Chapter Thirteen: Mastering Chatbots and Time Management

You can schedule ahead!! ☺ In my calendar, I will have marked down when I will send out information versus when I will send out content. Once a week, I set up my messages and then get back to income producing activities.

What kinds of messages do I set up?

In our particular business, we go live on a webinar a couple times a week. I know that my audience, which is typically parents and moms... are not checking their email when we start. Sending them... that "we are live" message... it does wonders EVERY time!

Also, since that is my typical audience, I send out my content at the times parents are most likely to be hanging around on social media. So, be sure to think through your audience. When are they available? When are they just hanging out browsing?

I have a google calendar you can attach to your calendar for a content and broadcast schedule. You can connect it to your calendar at www.TheBotIsInTheOffice.com

Also – remember, with the broadcast and sequence tools you can take care of a customer for weeks and weeks and weeks without ever having to touch the customer or the chatbot until they buy or become one of your students.

Most importantly though, start with a plan, think about your audience and know when the most effective time would be to communicate with them.

Chapter Fourteen: Why It's Easier Than Ever to Get Started with Mastering Chatbots

It's easier in the regard that there's more information out there, but as we all know, sometimes simple is better.

I wish I would have been able to find something that would have told me, "Okay, here is how you set it up, here's how to do a growth tool, here's how to do a broadcast and here's how to do a sequence."

Those are the main components of a chatbot that you want to master right away.

I also wish someone just said, "Here's all you need to do and here are some example scripts of what to send and what to say." Ha. I know that is wishful thinking, but that was what we needed. Since we could not find that, we built it.

But then we realized... we needed to know what to say... so we built that too. (See the back of the book for some examples you can use!)

Chapter Fifteen: Final Thoughts from Mastering Chatbots Expert Tarna Sadler

You have 20 minutes to start your chatbot. No, I'm just kidding, but yes, start right now.

The sooner you attach your chatbot to your page, the faster you're going to start getting subscribers.

Meaning, the minute somebody responds to a current messaging conversation, or the minute anybody sends you a message from your business page or opts-in, they're going to be a chatbot subscriber.

So, if you do nothing else, set it up!

It will start collecting your subscribers... even if you do nothing else with it... for now.

Do not what until you need it.

When the day comes, you can have an audience to communicate with in real time, quickly get their attention and, quickly move them through your decision-making process.

As we know and as we've seen in the few short years that chatbots have come into our life, they have grown immensely.

The landscape of our communication methods is going to continue to change.

This is a way for you to automate conversations, create a more interactive conversation and help your customers when they actually have the time to engage.

So instead of hiring an assistant or using your team's valuable time to respond to messages... master your chatbot and get back to living and saving.

I knew my alternative... it was either going to be me... or someone I was paying.

Chapter Sixteen: Where to Go from Here...

Did you know we have a number of detailed videos that will walk you through exactly what we show you in this book? Yep, it is true, and most of them are FREE.

You can register your book AND create a free account at www.TheBotIsInTheOffice.com

Join Tarna and family for exciting video lessons that make using chatbots in your own business easier, faster and more fun!

Go Here Now – www.TheBotIsInTheOffice.com

Until next time, Stay Legendary!

Tarna Sadler

"Normal Never Fit Us"

BONUSES!

CONTENT EXAMPLES

SCRIPT 1:

What's up?! We just released a NEW featured film showing off my 11-year-old digital entrepreneur...

It is a weekend coming up and it would be a great time to watch this with your kids!

 It is sure to get them inspired and get YOU inspired! And ... if you let it, it just may change your life!

Do you want to see the FULL episode?

ATTACH A SMALL (<25MB) VIDEO

Button – Take Me There

SCRIPT 2:

(Image below shows an option WITHOUT a button, and just a live link.)

Post

Good morning!! Here is a You Tube video I LOVE watching in the mornings. ♥ We all know... how our morning goes... shapes a lot of our day. This video helps me check into "me", before I check into "life".

https://youtu.be/QbAQemOMi1k

Enjoy! ♥

▷ Sent to	**420 people**	
⊘ Delivered to	**416**	99.0%
◉ Opened by	**413**	99.3%
👆 Clicked by	**0**	0%

SCRIPT 3:

WEBBIE REMINDER

Post

Hey `First Name`, are you free tonight by chance? We are doing a live overview of our business in about 45 minutes. :)

If you are free, you should come see us :)

I wanna watch :)	CTR 5%	>
Not free tonight!	CTR 9%	>

▷ Sent to	**424 people**	
⊘ Delivered to	**420**	99.1%
◉ Opened by	**418**	99.5%
👆 Clicked by	**59**	14.0%

SCRIPT 4:

Post

You asked for it!! Here you go!

We are live in 5 mins :)

Here is where you join 🔗

Watch Live!   CTR 44%

Sent to
▷ 18 people

Delivered to
⊘ 18   100.0%

Opened by
👁 18   100.0%

Clicked by
👆 8   44.4%

SCRIPT 5:

Webinar Replay Script: w/tags (send replay link)

Life Hacking LIVE pre-party starts today at 6p PST! So, check it out...
our speaker's tonight aren't the "normal" webcast speakers...

we have ACTUAL life hackers (like you're gonna be) who are KILLING it
in their (sometimes strange) ways...

Button

 I want to watch

SCRIPT 6:

Webinar Replay Script 2

I've got bad news.... :(

Last Monday night's webcast recordings disappear FOREVER tonight.

Did you get a chance to register your name and email?

If you have, you are one of the lucky few who can still see the most
valuable webcast we have done.

If you haven't yet, then this is the LAST WARNING. At midnight we are
pulling down the recording forever.

Button Title Examples:

Still Need to Register (send to lead capture page)

I Registered (send response with webinar page link/or send directly to webinar replay page link)

SCRIPT 7:

EBOOK Distribution

"wait a minute...you have an ebook?"

(Apparently, a lot of people were shocked by what I shared with them, so I had to give you a shot at it too)

...many....many people tell me these are the secrets they have been searching for....(you'll have to let me know what you think)

Buttons

I want a copy!

Tell me more... (share a brief bullet point list of what they'll learn in your ebook.)

SCRIPT 8:

BLOG

Did you know that there is nothing else that has as tangible of an ROI as...

spending each and every day the way you want?

Click below and I'll send you 15 more reasons why you need this in your life too. And, 10 ways to take control of your destiny now.

Button - Show me the 15!

Non-Bloggers...(Send them to a video of you sharing this info. (Either a landing page or directly send YT video)

SCRIPT 9:

SEQUENCE FOR BUSINESS PAGE INVITE, FRIEND REQUEST OR GROUP INVITE EXAMPLE

(Send three days after they subscribe)

Hey First Name, again I wanted to thank you for reaching out yesterday.

I wanted to invite you to see that I am a real person. Eek!! Who would've known?

No really, I'd love to keep in touch with you and continue to introduce you to a lifestyle by your design.

Come say hi ;)

Button - Add Me on FB

Add in your personal profile link | business page link | group page

SCRIPT 10:

Post

Hey friend, would you like to check out our Facebook group?

Together we support those who want to transition out of their 9-5 work week and into full-time freedom.

Come get inspired and motivated to live life on your terms! ·

Just tap the button below, and I will take care of the rest.

| Yes 🌟 | CTR 11% | > |

Sent to
▷ 245 people

Delivered to
⊘ 243   99.2%

Opened by
👁 234   96.3%

Clicked by
👆 27   11.1%

In closing, from my mom, whom had front row seats to my wildly crazy journey.

Wrinkled or creased, she was always there. And, with that, I hope you find the same.

My daughter through my eyes, ever since you were a preschool child you encouraged me by always wanting to help someone figure out a better way to do things, always wanting to be at the front of the line, yes being number one! I could see then leadership qualities then and there, beginning to blossom. All the way through your schooling you stepped up to the plate and took control of how you handled your homework, participated in family gatherings and always had time for your brothers and sisters! When you decided you were going to take the leap and become an online entrepreneur, I watched you dig in and join webinar after webinar, participate in reviewing the lessons and digging deeper, each and every time you had a question. Before I knew it in a matter of like three or four months the next thing I know you're coaching people towards the same idea. I remember the day your first check came in the mail, you were so very excited. It's seeming to put you into overdrive, because it became real, yes, a real check in the mail made out to you to build your empire. Within a few months you sold your home packed up and moved to out-of-state and launch yourself deeper into learning what it takes to be an online executive. Your first launch was self-branded and then one day led to the next and I watched the birthing of corporate escape artist aka CEA, when your first 10k month jumped out at you, YOU grabbed another gear. In your moments I stand back and watch and hear you coaching, directing, encouraging, guiding and loving on your team! I hear them say how excited they are to have you as a coach. Then I take a look out over our family life, and what are you doing next, homeschooling your son. It's awesome to see you work with him and be his teacher. I'm sure that he will flourish right alongside of you, why, because not only are you homeschooling him, you are taking the time to teach him about online business strategies on how and what to do. Watch out world, when it comes time for him to step up to bat, he'll be more than prepared and ready to rock. And in my heart and say Yep that's my daughter. I wish you the best of everything in this endeavor, I enjoy supporting you and watching you grow. May the Lord bless and keep you, stay legendary.